Ira Aldridge

Celebrated 19th Century Actor

Martin Hoyles

HANSIB PUBLICATIONS LTD
London and Hertfordshire UK

Published by Hansib Publications in 2008
London & Hertfordshire

Hansib Publications Limited
P.O. Box 226, Hertford, Hertfordshire, SG14 3WY, UK

Email: info@hansib-books.com
Website: www.hansib-books.com

ISBN 978-1-870518-92-5

Printed and bound by The Alden Press, Oxford, UK

To Asher and Rosa, with all my love

Books by the author

The Politics of Literacy, Writers & Readers Publishing Cooperative 1977

Changing Childhood, Writers & Readers Publishing Cooperative 1979

More Valuable Than Gold by Striking Miners' Children, Hoyles 1985

The Politics of Childhood, Journeyman 1989

The Story of Gardening, Journeyman 1991

Gardeners Delight: Gardening Books from 1560 to 1960, Volume 1, Pluto 1994

Bread and Roses: Gardening Books from 1560 to 1960, Volume 2, Pluto 1995

The Gardener's Perpetual Almanack, Thames & Hudson 1997

Remember Me: Achievements of Mixed-Race People, Past & Present (with Asher Hoyles), Hansib 1999

Moving Voices: Black Performance Poetry (with Asher Hoyles), Hansib 2002

The Axe Laid to the Root: The Story of Robert Wedderburn, Hansib 2004

Dyslexia from a Cultural Perspective (with Asher Hoyles), Hansib 2007

Acknowledgements

Many thanks to the following people for their invaluable help in producing this book: Arif Ali, Kash Ali, Richard Painter and Isha Persaud at Hansib Publications, Shango Baku, Ruth Cowhig, Krystyna Kujawinska Courtney, Oku Ekpenyon, Ray Fearon, Beata Gradowska, Bernth Lindfors, Susan Skedd, Hazel Waters.

Picture Credits

Bakrushin State Central Theatrical Museum, Moscow, 58, 65, 70; Harvard Theatre Collection, 60; Kiev State Museum, 78; Manchester Art Gallery, portrait entitled 'Othello, the Moor of Venice' by James Northcote, front cover; Museum of the City of New York, 45; Russian State Museum of Theatrical, Musical and Cinematographical Art, 81, 88; Schomburg Collection, 43, 70.

Contents

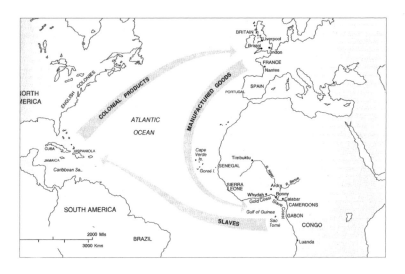

Map showing Senegal and the 'triangular trade' in slaves

Drawing of Ira Aldridge as a boy, from *Actor in Exile* by Mary Malone

Childhood

Ira Aldridge was one of the most celebrated actors of the nineteenth century. He performed in all the major towns in England, Ireland, Scotland and Wales, and he won international fame when he toured the continent of Europe, earning a dozen honours and awards, including a knighthood in Germany. He was most famous for his portrayal of Othello in Shakespeare's play, but he also acted in many other roles in a career spanning more than forty years.

> **"Mislike me not for my complexion,**
> **The shadowed livery of the burnished sun,**
> **To whom I am a neighbour and near bred."**
> Prince of Morocco, in Shakespeare's *Merchant of Venice* 1595

> **"Is black so base a hue?"**
> Aaron, in Shakespeare's *Titus Andronicus* 1594

> **"Look on me. Who am I? I know, thou say'st,**
> **The Moor, a slave, an abject, beaten slave:**
> **Eternal woes to him that made me so!**
> **But look again. Has six years cruel bondage**
> **Extinguish'd majesty so far, that nought**
> **Shines here to give an awe of one above thee?"**
> Zanga, in Edward Young's *The Revenge* 1721

Ira Frederick Aldridge was born in New York on 24 July 1807. His father Daniel was also born in New York City and his mother Luranah came from the

Mariama Ba

state of Delaware. He had an older brother Joshua and a younger sister Susannah, whom he later supported financially when her husband was ill and she had a family of small children.

Ira stated that they were descended from the Fulah people of Senegal. The Fulah, or Peulh, are spread throughout west Africa, but make up only a minority of the population of Senegal. Some of Ira's ancestors, however, may well have found themselves sold into slavery and transported across the Atlantic, via the slave house on Gorée Island. The famous Senegalese novelist, Mariama Ba, also belongs to this ethnic group.

His parents were free Blacks. This meant that they were not slaves, but still generally had to do

The Slave House on Gorée Island, off the coast of Dakar, Senegal, with the Gateway of No Return in the centre of the picture.

labouring jobs. In 1820 there were about 500 slaves in New York and 10,000 free Blacks. Ira's father sometimes worked as a grain measurer and more often sold straw from a cart. He was also a lay preacher in Old Zion, the African Church in the city.

When Ira was ten years old, his mother died and his father remarried. Ira decided to run away and sailed south to North Carolina, which was a slave state. A slave-dealer offered 500 dollars for the boy, but the captain refused, saying he had promised to take him back to New York.

The Gateway of No Return in the Slave House, through which slaves walked along a plank to the ship that would transport them across the Atlantic

New York African Free School

The school Ira attended was one of the African Free Schools in the city. These were sponsored by the Quakers and first set up in 1787. The schools were to produce many of the African Americans who campaigned against slavery, for example Henry Highland Garnet. They were known as Abolitionists.

One of his teachers was Mr. Andrews, a White man, who encouraged his dramatic talent. He was "awarded prizes for declamation, in which he excelled". His brother Joshua said of him: "Ira, being a somewhat intelligent lad, was held in considerable favor for his quickness and attention to his studies, both by his teacher and his schoolmates."

James McCune Smith   **Henry Highland Garnet**

One of his schoolmates was James McCune Smith, who later qualified as a doctor and became one of the leaders of the abolitionist movement. In a *Memoir*, published in 1860, he records the way Ira ran away from home and adds: "Shortly after his return home, Brown's Theatre was opened and Ira, with his brother Joshua, took to the stage; but their father, finding it out, took them away from the theatre."

Love of Theatre

**"The young Roscius hung about the 'wings',
receiving intoxicating pleasure, listening with
rapture to the wildest rant, and strengthening
his hopes of emulating the most admired actors
who presented themselves."** *Memoir* 1849

"So foul and fair a day I have not seen."
Macbeth, in Shakespeare's *Macbeth* 1606

**"Dear heart, what a terrible life am I led!
A dog has better, that's sheltered and fed."**
Mungo, in Isaac Bickerstaffe's *The Padlock* 1768

At this time most theatres in the USA denied admission to Black people, but Ira managed to watch from the wings of the Chatham Theatre, where he used to help some of the actors with their costumes. He was also allowed to sit in the balcony of the Park Theatre which had a capacity of 2,500. Here he saw a number of English actors perform in Shakespeare's plays.

A *Memoir*, published much later, recorded: "His first visit to a theatre fixed the great purpose of his life, and established the sole end and aim of his existence. He would be an actor. He says at this hour that he was bewildered, amazed, dazzled, fascinated, by what to him was splendour beyond all that his mind had imagined, and mimic life so captivating, that his own real existence

James Hewlett as Richard III

would be worthless unless he in some way participated in such imitations as he witnessed."

There was one theatre in New York, however, which Ira could comfortably visit. This was the African Grove Theatre, the first ever Black American theatre, set up in 1821, six years before slavery was outlawed in New York state. Its founder was William Alexander Brown, a retired West Indian steamship steward, who also worked as a tailor.

Brown converted part of his property into a 300-seat theatre, where Shakespeare was performed, as well as pantomime and farce. A separate section was set aside at the back for White audience members because, in the words of the theatre's management, "Whites do not know how to conduct themselves at entertainments for ladies and gentlemen of color".

The African Theatre Company was directed by the Black actor James Hewlett, whom Ira came to know and admire. Hewlett acted the Shakespearean parts of Othello and Richard III, and clearly inspired the young Ira. The company, however, was often harassed by the police and it faced hostility from the White population, so it had to move several times to different venues. This was a time when doors in New York had signs up saying "Dogs and Negroes Forbidden". On 19 July, 1822, Aldridge himself was assaulted on the street and severely beaten up by James Bellmont, a circus performer.

Pizarro

The pro-slavery sheriff of New York, Mordecai Manual Noah, who was also a lawyer, judge and newspaper editor, pursued Brown, "closing performance after performance, making some arrests right off the stage. The arrests became so commonplace that the actors continued performing, even in the jail cells."

With some friends and with great determination, Ira put on a production of *Pizarro*, Sheridan's version of a play by Kotzebue. Significantly he took the part of the hero Rolla, the Peruvian leader who challenged the Spanish invaders. It was to be followed by *Romeo and*

Juliet, but White jealousy of their success led to riots, probably organised by Stephen Price, the owner of the nearby Park Theatre.

The gallery in the Park Theatre, reserved for Black spectators, held 750 people, so when they decided to attend the Grove instead, Price lost money. The final riot was caused by a gang of about fifteen to twenty ruffians who entered the theatre and smashed it up, attacking actors and actresses and beating up manager Brown. The police then closed the theatre for good.

Travel to England

"Coal-black is better than another hue,
In that it scorns to bear another hue."
Aaron, in Shakespeare's *Titus Andronicus* 1594

"His mere presence on the English stage
was proof of the ability of Blacks to achieve
parity with Whites in the performing arts,
and by extension in all areas of endeavour,
given the necessary education and training."
Errol G. Hill & James V. Hatch, *A History of African American Theatre* 2003

"I love her! Yes, this man whose face is black,
this man who was once a slave, dares to love
a white maiden, the daughter of his master.
Oh, he is mad!"
Fabian, in *The Black Doctor* 1846

After three years of amateur dramatics, Ira realised that there was no future for him as an actor in America, so in 1824, at the age of seventeen, he left for England. He worked his passage to Liverpool as a ship's steward.

Amazingly, in May 1825, when still only seventeen years old, Aldridge was performing as Othello at the Royalty Theatre in the east end of London. In the space of a month he played several other roles in that theatre, including that of Gambia in *The Slave*.

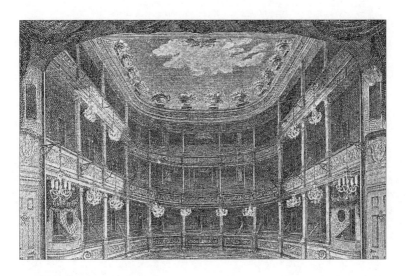

The Royalty Theatre

By October he had moved to a larger theatre, the Royal Coburg (now the Old Vic) in south London. There he played the part of the African prince Oroonoko in *The Revolt of Surinam*, a dramatisation by the Irish playwright Thomas Southerne of Aphra Behn's novel *Oroonoko* which she wrote in 1696. It was a story which challenged the evils of slavery and the production was a remarkable success, despite a racist review in *The Times* which said that "owing to the shape of his lips it is utterly impossible for him to pronounce English"!

In September of that year, Ira had met Margaret Gill, a Yorkshire woman from Northallerton. She was ten years older than him and was the daughter of a stocking weaver. They were married on 27 November at St. George's Church in Bloomsbury, London. On the marriage certificate

The Royal Coburg Theatre, now the Old Vic

The Old Vic, 2007

his name is written as Frederick William Aldridge, so it may be that Ira was originally a nickname. It was not until 1833 that his name began appearing on playbills as Ira Aldridge.

In his *Memoir* of 1860, his school friend, James McCune Smith, describes Margaret as "an intelligent lady", who "had made a runaway match with the African Roscius. She was a lady of fine accomplishments and great conversational talent." Aldridge's marriage to a White woman would not have endeared him to London racists! In his lifetime he also had affairs with other White women, which would have added fuel to the racist fire.

Marriage certificate for Ira Aldridge and Margaret Gill

In the same year, in December, Ira played Othello again, this time at the Theatre Royal, Brighton. It was to be his most famous role and there are many pictures of him playing this part. Already, this early in his career, the review in the *Brighton Gazette* was complimentary, calling him

Margaret Gill

"an actor of real and undoubted talent", and adding, "although his voice was loud and energetic, his style was perfectly free from extravagance; his action on the contrary chaste, and his attitudes generally appropriate and graceful." He was "received with great applause".

The summer of the following year, 1826, found Aldridge in Exeter appealing for financial help, "both himself and his wife being in deep distress". Yet in the same year he had his portrait painted by James Northcote, a member of the Royal Academy and one of the most famous portrait painters of the time. The artist described it as 'The Head of a Negro in the Character of Othello'. Northcote, then eighty years old, was earlier a pupil of Joshua Reynolds, and exhibited with both Reynolds and Turner. It was clearly a great honour.

Auditorium of the Royal Coburg Theatre

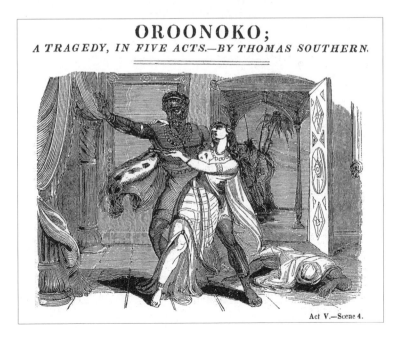

Oroonooko

**Painting of Ira Aldridge as Othello,
by Henry Perronet Briggs**

The painting, now entitled 'Othello, the Moor of Venice', is on display in Manchester Art Gallery and forms the cover of this book. In February 1827, Aldridge performed in six different plays, including *Othello*, at the Theatre Royal, Manchester, and later in the year his portrait was exhibited at the Royal Manchester Institution. It was praised as "the best executed painting in the exhibition" and purchased. Northcote received thirty guineas for it, which today would be worth several thousand pounds. It was appropriate that the Institution bought the work, as Manchester was one of the centres of the movement to abolish slavery.

A few years later he was painted again, by another leading portrait painter of the time, Henry Perronet Briggs. Entitled 'Ira Frederick Aldridge as Othello', the portrait was completed in about 1830. After the death of Northcote in 1831, Briggs was elected to the Royal Academy.

In 1827 Aldridge also received his first official recognition, from the Government of the Republic of Haiti, who honoured "the first man of colour in the theatre" with a commission in the army. This was delivered to him through the Consul in London. It was significant that this honour should come from the Black republic set up by ex-slaves, who had successfully fought for their freedom, led by Toussaint L'Ouverture. This rebellion was to be one of the main catalysts in ending slavery in the nineteenth century.

Toussaint L'Ouverture

Othello

**"Speak of me as I am; nothing extenuate,
Nor set down ought in malice."**
Othello, in Shakespeare's *Othello* 1604

**"Othello in the Venice of that time was in
practically the same position as a coloured
man in America today."**
Paul Robeson *London Interview* 1930

In Shakespeare's play, Othello is described as "a
noble Moor; in the service of the Venetian state".
He is a soldier and in his own account of his past
exploits he speaks of having been "sold to
slavery". In the play, however, he leads the defeat
of the Turks in Cyprus and is referred to as "our
noble and valiant general". Nevertheless the play
is full of the racist comments of the other
characters. Roderigo calls him a "lascivious
Moor"; Brabantio refers to him as a "thing" with a
"sooty bosom"; Iago describes him as an "erring
barbarian" and a "devil" who tells "fantastical lies".

It is not surprising that the play appealed so
much to Aldridge. It revealed the prevalent racism,
but in acting out the tragedy of the noble Moor,
Aldridge turned it into a victory on the stage. A
review in *The Times* (26 March 1848) indicates how
he put his heart and soul into the part: "In the sense
of emotion, Mr. Aldridge is exceedingly natural; his
grief and joy seem to spring from his heart."

Ira Aldridge as Othello in St. Petersburg, 1858

William Wells Brown

William Wells Brown, who had escaped from slavery and who became one of the greatest anti-slavery campaigners in Britain, when he spent five years touring the country, saw Aldridge play Othello. In his book *The Black Man: His Antecedents, His Genius, and His Achievements*, published in 1863, he describes the effect the actor had before he had even started acting: "All eyes are turned to the right door, and thunders of applause greet the appearance of Othello. Mr. Aldridge is of the middle size, and appeared to be about three quarters African; has a pleasant countenance, frame well knit, and seemed to me the best Othello that I had ever seen." At the end of the play, he adds: "The audience with one impulse rose to its feet amid the wildest enthusiasm. Othello was called before the curtain and received the applause of the delighted multitude."

Brown also records seeing Aldridge play Hamlet: "The following evening I went to witness his Hamlet, and was surprised to find him as perfect in that as he had been in Othello; for I had been led to believe that the latter was his greatest character. The voice was so low, and sad, and sweet, the modulation so tender, the dignity so natural, the grace so consummate, that all yielded themselves silently to the delicious enchantment. I thought Hamlet one of his best characters, though I saw him afterwards in several others."

Racism

Just as Othello experienced racism in Venice, and Ira Aldridge in New York, so he underwent a similar experience in London. This was a period of intense political debate about human rights. Abolitionists were fighting for the ending of slavery in the West Indies and America.

Harriet Martineau, English feminist and abolitionist, toured all over the USA between 1834 and 1836 and noted in her book *Society in America* (1837) the "eight hundred flourishing abolition societies of the north". She also commented on the dangers the abolitionists faced: "The governor of South Carolina last year recommended the summary execution of all persons caught within the limits of the State, holding avowed anti-slavery opinions."

By the middle of the century there were 3 million slaves in the USA. Harriet Tubman (c. 1820-

Harriet Tubman

1913), who had escaped slavery at the age of twenty-five, was helping slaves travel to freedom in Canada on her Underground Railroad. Sojourner Truth (c. 1797-1883) was freed from slavery in 1827 and proceeded to lecture at anti-slavery meetings in over twenty states of the USA. Frederick Douglass (1817-1895) escaped from slavery in 1838 and became the most famous American anti-slavery campaigner. Along with William Wells Brown and Ellen and William Craft, all escaped slaves, Douglass gave anti-slavery lectures all over Britain to audiences of thousands.

Frederick Douglass

Ellen and William Craft

With the passing of the Fugitive Slave Act in 1850, escaped slaves could be caught and returned to their masters in the south. In *Incidents in the Life of a Slave Girl*, published in 1861, Harriet Jacobs describes the reign of terror which followed: "Many a wife discovered a secret she had never known before – that her husband was a fugitive, and must leave her to ensure his own safety. Worse still, many a husband discovered that his wife had fled from slavery years ago, and as 'the child follows the condition of its mother', the children of his love were liable to be seized and carried into slavery."

People were also concerned about the oppressive nature of the Government in Britain. In 1819, 80,000 people had assembled in St. Peter's Fields, Manchester to demand reform. The yeomanry charged the crowd and within minutes eleven people were killed and over 400 wounded. Within two days the whole of the country knew of Peterloo. The poet Shelley heard about it in Italy and wrote his famous condemnation *The Mask of Anarchy*:

Rise like Lions after slumber
In unvanquishable number,
Shake your chains to earth like dew
Which in sleep had fallen on you –
Ye are many – they are few.

The following year five men were hanged for a plot (known as the Cato Street Conspiracy) to assassinate the prime minister and his whole

THEATRE-ROYAL, BRISTOL.

Nights of Performing this Week

MONDAY, TUESDAY, THURSDAY & FRIDAY.

Second Appearance of the African Tragedian,

MR. IRA ALDRIDGE,

(From the Theatre-Royal, Covent Garden and London Theatres), the far-famed

African Roscius,

WHO IS ENGAGED FOR

FIVE NIGHTS ONLY,

And whose recent Performances on the London Stage have received the most flattering eulogies of the Public Press, without exception, and witnessed by Crowded and Delighted Audiences with the greatest possible Enthusiasm,

On MONDAY, March 18th, 1850,

Will be presented Shakspear's sublime Tragedy of

OTHELLO,

MOOR OF VENICE.

Othello - - - - - **by the AFRICAN ROSCIUS**

Iago .... Mr. COLEMAN
Brabantio .... Mr. MADDOCKS | Roderigo .... Mr. GOMERSAL
Cassio .... Mr. JOHN DAVIS
Montano .... Mr. LEE | Ludovico .... Mr. SUMMERS | Duke of Venice .... Mr. ELMORE
Julio .... Mr. ANDREWS | Gratiano .... Mr. MULFORD
Luca ...... Mr. WALDRON | Antonio ...... Mr. CALLAN | Messenger ...... Mr. ADAMS | Paulo ...... Mr. NELSON
Desdemona .... Mrs. MADDOCKS | Emilia .... Mrs. ELMORE

Pas Seul - - - - **Miss BEAUFORT.**

To conclude with the Laughable Farce of

THE PADLOCK.

Don Diego .... Mr. SUMMERS, in which Character he will sing
"Thoughts to Council," and "By some I'm told."
Leander .... Mr. BOMER, in which Character he will sing
"I Love her," and "Lady mine."
First Scholar .... Mr. K. W. WALDRON | Second Scholar .... Mr. NELSON

Mungo - - - - - - - **by the AFRICAN ROSCIUS**
Who has been universally acknowledged one of the most perfect Delineations of the Negro Character
on the Stage; in which he will sing
"Dear Heart, what a terrible Life I'm led," "Opossum up a Gum Tree,"
and "Negro Boy."
Leonora .... Miss CUTHBERT, in which she will sing the Song of
"Lovely Night."
Ursula .... Miss CARHE.

Tuesday, FATHER and SON; Ameline, by the *African Roscius.* After which, CHARLES TWELFTH.
To conclude with the VIRGINIAN MUMMY; Ginger Blue, by the *African Roscius.*

Dress Boxes, 4s. Half-price, 2s.; Upper Boxes, 3s.; Half-price, 1s. 6d.; Pit, 2s. Half-price, 1s.; Gallery, 1s.
Private and Places for the Boxes to be taken of Mr. HIGGS, at the Theatre, from Eleven till Three o'Clock.
Doors open at Half-past Six. Performance commence at Seven.

Half-Price to the Gallery. Quarter before Nine—SIXPENCE.

Parties desirous of having Bills supplied, will confer great favour by giving information to the Box Book-keeper, at Theatre
Leader, Mrs. WORKADY. Leader of the Band, Mr. T. SALMON. Stage Manager, Mr. JOHN DAVIS.

Somerton Printer, Mercury Office, Broad Street.

Ira Aldridge playing Othello and Mungo in Bristol, 1850

cabinet. One of them was a Black man, born in Jamaica, called William Davidson. Also in 1820, Robert Wedderburn, another Jamaican living in London, was sentenced to two years in prison, supposedly for blasphemy, but really for preaching revolution and freedom for the slaves in the West Indies. The Home Secretary called him a "notorious firebrand" and his oratory was so powerful that he was put on the Government's secret list of 33 leading reformers.

In 1824, the year Aldridge arrived in England, trade unions were finally legalised. But in 1834 six farm labourers from Dorset were sentenced to transportation to Australia for forming a trade union. They became known as the Tolpuddle Martyrs. Two years later the Chartist Movement began, the largest political movement in Britain's history, demanding reform of parliament. In 1842 they presented a petition signed by over 3 million people, well over half the adult male population of Great Britain. One of their leaders was William Cuffay, a Black tailor, whose militancy led to a sentence of transportation to Tasmania in 1848.

Although Britain had officially ended the slave trade in 1807, slavery itself was only declared abolished in the British Empire in 1833, to be enacted on 1 August 1834. There were still many people in Britain who thought the slaves were not ready for emancipation, as indeed William Wilberforce had earlier stated. Not so the slaves in Jamaica, however, where in 1831 there took place the greatest slave uprising the British Caribbean had ever seen. It was led by Samuel Sharpe, who stated, "I would rather die upon yonder gallows than live in slavery." Just as Oroonoko, whom Aldridge played many times, declared:

'tis nobler to die,
Than drag the galling yoke of slavery.

Many people in Britain thought Black people were inherently inferior. They could not or would not accept that Ira Aldridge was a brilliant Shakespearean actor. All through his career he would show through his achievements what a Black man could do – against all the odds! He was a living refutation of the racists' argument.

It is significant that he was called the 'African Roscius' after the most famous Roman actor Quintus Roscius Gallus, a slave who taught Cicero how to speak in public. He was born around 126 BC and died in 62 BC, and was celebrated for his acting both in tragedy and comedy. The name was a traditional compliment in the English-speaking theatre. Richard Burbage (1566-1619), the celebrated actor of Shakespeare's times, was known as 'England's great Roscius', and the most famous actor of the eighteenth century, David Garrick (1717-1779), was called the 'British Roscius'.

Banned from London Theatres

"Their attacks on Aldridge grew more virulent as their position grew indefensible, and the appearance of a Negro playing the finest roles in all drama on the boards of Covent Garden was itself a damning negation, as Aldridge well knew, of their arguments and 'theories' about the so-called inferior races. Aldridge stood upon the stage as the lone protagonist of his oppressed and vilified people."
Herbert Marshall & Mildred Stock *Ira Aldridge: The Negro Tragedian 1958*

"If you prick us, do we not bleed?"
Shylock, in Shakespeare's *Merchant of Venice* 1595

"Single-handedly, and with great determination, Aldridge gave the lie to the racist assumptions of English society."
Hazel Waters *Aldridge and the Battlefield of Race* 2003

In April 1833 there was an attempt to stop Aldridge playing Othello at the Theatre Royal in Covent Garden. Edmund Kean was due to play the part, but collapsed on the opening night and died a few weeks later. Aldridge was asked to take over, but a vicious campaign was mounted to stop him, with *The Athenaeum* describing it as "monstrous" for an authentic Black to appear in the play: "In the name of propriety and decency we protest against

Edmund Kean as Othello

an interesting actress and decent girl like Miss Ellen Tree being subjected by the manager of a theatre to the indignity of being pawed about by Mr. Wallack's black servant."

This was the year that Britain abolished slavery in its colonies, but the act was not passed in parliament until 31 July and did not become law until 29 August. The Society of West India

William Lloyd Garrison

Merchants and Planters was still very active, through its literary committee, publishing propaganda in favour of slavery. It bought space in *The Times* and many other newspapers to publicise its views. There was also a big debate about paying compensation – not to the slaves, but to the owners! This was the same year in which William Lloyd Garrison formed the American Anti-Slavery Society.

Friends and supporters of Aldridge rallied to his defence and produced a handbill:

Base and unmanly attempts are making in certain quarters to prevent MR. ALDRIDGE, commonly designated the 'African Roscius' from making his appearance as OTHELLO, on Wednesday next, pursuant to his engagement at the Theatre Royal, Covent Garden, or if he should have the 'PRESUMPTION' to appear, he is threatened with DAMNATION!

His heinous offence is, that he was born in Africa, and though 'descended from a line of Kings', his skin is too DARK to enable him to personate the 'DUSKY MOOR', even though he may possess the genius of Kean, the classic taste of a Kemble, combined with the dramatic experience of a Garrick!!

Aldridge did play the part, but only for two performances. After that he was effectively banned from acting in the major London theatres and so he undertook a tour of the provinces.

He did return later to perform in the West End, at the Lyceum Theatre in 1858 and the Haymarket Theatre in 1865, both times as Othello. By this time *The Athenaeum* had changed its tune. In 1858 it noted that Aldridge "not only spoke

Playbill announcing Mr. Aldridge, a native of Senegal

distinctly and correctly, but with elocutional emphasis and propriety… his general action marked with elegance and ease." And in 1865: "Altogether we have seldom witnessed a representation of this great tragedy which pleases us more."

Tour of the Country

"We dance and we sing,
Till we make a house ring
And, tied in his garters, old massa may swing."
Mungo, in Isaac Bickerstaffe's *The Padlock* 1768

"Let Europe and her pallid sons go weep;
Let Afric and her hundred thrones rejoice:
Oh, my dear countrymen, look down, and see
How I bestride your prostrate conqueror!
I tread on haughty Spain, and all her kings."
Zanga, in Edward Young's *The Revenge* 1721

"I can see far into the future – can behold the
time when white and black shall be of equal
worth." Dred, in W. E. Suter's *Dred: A Tale of the
Dismal Swamp* 1856

Soon after arriving in England, Aldridge had
made his first tour of the country. In 1827 he
performed in Sheffield, Halifax, Manchester,
Newcastle, Edinburgh, Lancaster, Liverpool
and Sunderland.

In 1831 he was in Ireland performing *Othello*
in Dublin. The great actor Edmund Kean saw him
and "complimented him highly". Kean also wrote
a letter of introduction for Aldridge to the manager
of the Theatre Royal in Bath: "This introduces to
you the African Roscius – he is excessively clever
in general but I look upon his Mungo as one of the
first pieces of acting on the British Stage."

Ira Aldridge as Aaron the Moor in *Titus Andronicus*, 1852

Edmund Kean as Richard III

On a later tour of Scotland in 1848, his portrayal of Othello in Dundee was praised by the *Arbroath Guide* as "a perfect performance such as we venture to say could not be surpassed. We have had the pleasure of seeing Kean the Elder, Young, Macready, and other tragedians of celebrity in this part, but great as these were, as a whole we prefer Mr. Aldridge's impersonation of the Moor to that of any actor we ever saw."

As well as performing great tragic roles, Aldridge was also skilled at playing comedy, in particular the part of Mungo in *The Padlock*, an eighteenth-century play by the Irish playwright Isaac Bickerstaffe. The story, based on *The Jealous*

**Engraving of Ira Aldridge as Mungo
in *The Padlock***

Husband by Cervantes, is about a rich West Indian planter called Don Diego, who locks up his young intended wife and leaves the key to her door with his house slave, the impertinent and mischievous Mungo, with strict instructions to allow no one to enter the house while he is away. As soon as he is gone, Mungo helps himself to a bottle of liquor, sings anti-slavery songs, and admits the lady's lover to her room.

The play gave Aldridge an opportunity to display his talents in playing the guitar, singing and dancing, as well as acting. A review in *The Times* (26 March 1848) said: "Mr Aldridge played

Obi, or Three Fingered Jack

the part of the Negro servant with extraordinary humour and natural drollery." *The Padlock* became a regular part of his repertoire and he also produced it on tour in Europe. In Russia he included Russian folksongs in the performance, which he sang in the original language.

Several melodramas appeared regularly in Aldridge's repertoire. One was *Dred: A Tale of the Dismal Swamp* by W. E. Suter, based on a novel by Harriet Beecher Stowe. The main character, however, is the opposite of Uncle Tom. Dred declares: "Oh, that all slaves would revolt, and so destroy the curse of this fair land."

The Black Doctor

Another was *Obi, or Three-fingered Jack*, about a fugitive slave seeking revenge. The story is based on Jack Mansong, or Three Finger Jack - so named because he lost two fingers in a fight. He was an escaped slave, whose monument in Jamaica records, "He fought, often singlehandedly, a war of terror against the English soldiers and planters who held the slave colony. Strong, brave, skilled with machete and musket, his bold exploits were equalled only by his chivalry. He loved his country and his people."

He was eventually ambushed and killed in 1781. His life became a legend and several books

Ira Aldridge as Zanga in *The Revenge*

and plays were written about him. In England the play started off as a pantomime, but in the late 1820s a theatre manager in Edinburgh, named William Murray, rewrote it "expressly" for Aldridge, as a melodrama.

He included in the text a powerful denunciation of the slave-traders, spoken by Jack: "I had a daughter once, did they spare her harmless infancy? Where is my wife? Was she spared to me? No! with blood and rapine the white man swept like a hurricane o'er our native village, and blasted every hope! Can aught efface the terrible remembrance from my soul, how at their lordly feet

Surrey Theatre

we begged for mercy and found it not. Our women knelt, our infants shrieked in vain, as the blood-stained murderer ranged from hut to hut, dragging the husband and the father from their homes, to sell them into bondage! No more, no more! The vext spirits of my wife and child hover o'er me like a holy curse, and claim this due revenge."

Aldridge wrote some of his own material too. He adapted Shakespeare's *Titus Andronicus* quite fundamentally, turning the villain, Aaron the Moor, into a hero! He also adapted a French play *The Black Doctor*, about a mixed-race doctor who marries the daughter of an aristocratic White

Auditorium of the Surrey Theatre, 1849

family. It enabled Aldridge to perform in another play about a mixed marriage, similar to *Othello* and *Oroonoko*.

On the closing night of a performance at a given theatre Aldridge would talk to the audience directly in what was known as a farewell address. He would speak about the injustice and cruelty of slavery and of the passionate desire for freedom of all those held in bondage.

After a performance as Zanga the Moor in Edward Young's *The Revenge* at the Surrey Theatre, for example, Aldridge was called for on

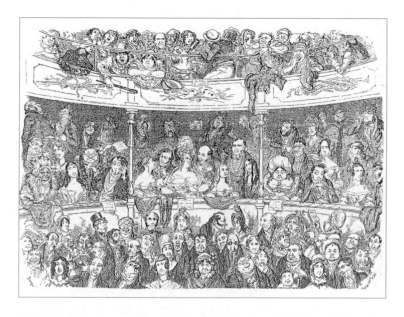

Cruickshank drawing of the pit, boxes and gallery of the Surrey Theatre, 1836

stage. According to a report, he made an eloquent address and stated that "the twenty years' struggle he had made was amply repaid by the reception he had that night received, and hoped the prejudice was fast dying away, when one man should be deprived of a hearing on the stage, because his face was of another colour, seeing the black man and the white were both the work of the same Creator." His speech produced "the most deafening applause".

In 1833 one critic explained the appeal of Zanga to Aldridge: "Dark and malevolent as he is represented, some sympathy is excited for him by the remembrance that his lofty and impatient spirit has been irritated by his father's death, his own

Drawing of Ira Aldridge as Zanga in *The Revenge*, from the *Illustrated London News*

conquest, captivity, loss of crown, and the indignity of the blow – all from the same person; against whom, an open and honourable atonement being impossible, he employs a subtle and secret vengeance. No wonder it appealed to the African Roscius."

A review of one of Aldridge's performances in the role appeared in the *Illustrated London News*, 1 April, 1848: "His reception throughout the performance was flattering; and, as the play progressed, the applause became enthusiastic. Mr. Aldridge possesses an excellent voice, commanding figure, and expressive countenance; to which he adds the advantages of education and study."

As well as speaking out against slavery, Aldridge also regularly sent money to the Negro State Conventions operating in America between 1830 and 1861. An article in the *Amsterdam News*, a New York Black daily newspaper, reported on 20 November 1943: "He sent back thousands of dollars to help his enslaved people and said many times that he could never be happy as long as one of his race was in chains."

A more contemporary account appeared in Russia in 1864: "Since the commencement of the struggle for the liberation of the blacks, the famous tragedian has donated half of his takings, i.e. of the money received from his performances, into the funds of an organisation for the work of freeing the slaves. Such a regular, voluntary deprival of half his own means of livelihood fully characterises his moral and civil development as a man and an artist." (*Information Bulletin of Saratov*, Number 141)

Tour of Europe

"Mr Ira Aldridge is, without exception,
the Greatest Stage Actor that ever lived."
Vienna

"It is truly wonderful to see an African treading
the boards of a theatre, in the part of Othello, in
which Mr Ira Aldridge is not to be surpassed."
Berlin

"Mr Ira Aldridge is most decidedly the greatest
Dramatic Artist we have ever seen. In the parts
of Othello, Macbeth and Shylock, he stands
unrivalled in our annals of the Stage."
Danzig

On 14 July 1852 Ira Aldridge left England, with his
wife and son, who was five years old, for a tour of
the continent. He was the manager and leading
actor of a small band of English actors and he was
to stay abroad for the next three years.

One of the first reports of his tour comes from
an event in Germany, which illustrates the power
and realism of his performance: "His acting and
mimicry in shattering scenes are incredible, and
certainly no one has understood Othello as well as
he. Once in Cologne, when, during the course of
the play he grasps Iago by the throat one of the
spectators shouted out, 'Kill the villain! Strangle

Ira Aldridge with his elder son, Ira Daniel

him!' Brought to himself by the general laughter of the audience, he rushed out of the theatre saying, 'Well, you just can't listen calmly to that actor!'"

In 1853 Aldridge first performed in Poland. A reviewer who saw him play Othello wrote: "His face, eyes, and lips portrayed his feelings even before he said anything. Each twitch of his facial or body muscles, each flash of his eyes revealed Othello's agitated heart, even if the spectators could not understand the language."

On this tour his wife looked after his son and also helped look after the money, as they were often swindled by theatre managements. A diary entry for 24 July 1854 relates how, in Rostock, he was serenaded for his birthday and treated with a barrel of beer.

Lithograph of Ira Aldridge by Barabas, 1853

The English theatre company soon disbanded, but Ira continued to perform with other actors who spoke the text in their own language. He would act in English and, as he had learnt some German and Russian, sometimes gave cues in these languages to help his fellow-actors.

On a later trip to Stockholm in 1857, he writes back to his wife explaining some of the problems

Ira Aldridge as Othello in Stockholm, 1857

of this method of performing: "As usual the leading man is grumbling about the disadvantage he says he will be at not understanding English. He forgets that I am at a greater disadvantage, his language is understood by the entire audience while I am partially so. However, that is easily got over."

In the same letter he shows his concern for his wife, who is ill, and also for his son who is now ten years old: "I trust that my dear Ira is well. I had a most unpleasant dream last night respecting him and awoke crying. I hope that he is attentive to you and I am sure that he is a good boy. Kisses for you and him and God Bless you both."

Ira Aldridge signs himself 'African Tragedian'

It is from Poland that we first hear of his financial contributions to the abolitionist cause in America and it is worth quoting the newspaper report in full:

"Though Ira Aldridge performs at present on the stage in Crakow, it is not from the things written about him as an actor that he will be remembered, but as a human being. The artistic triumphs which Ira Aldridge has gained in a few years throughout Europe are known to all; it would be unnecessary therefore to reiterate them. Less known, however, is how he uses in a noble and disinterested manner, the material gains from his triumphs. This artist has taken upon himself the task of showing Europe that his race is capable of educating itself, and not only by showing himself on the stage does he speak for the emancipation of the Negro, but also his actions are in the same spirit. Not long ago the Press brought news of a beautiful trend in his character which carries his name from mouth to mouth, and we are impelled to repeat it.

A Negro family called Wilson, a father, mother, son, and two daughters, fled from slavery in Baltimore and reached New York during the night. Nevertheless, through the Fugitive Slave Act of 1850, they were captured and arrested for the crime of demanding freedom; and it costs a lot to buy them out in the country of freedom. They were then put up for sale individually, the mother and father to be sent to the plantations of Georgia; both daughters were destined to a sad and degrading fate, which often befell fugitive slaves. The Society for the Manumission of Slaves in New York at the time had no funds to buy out the family, and Ira Aldridge, playing at that time in Austria, had learned from the English Press of this incident, and at once sent to New York the money needed to buy the freedom of this family. In this way does Ira Aldridge use his earnings."
Czasu 3 November 1854

Stadt=Theater zu Leipzig.

Freitag, den 26. November 1852.

Abonnement suspendu.

Erstdarstellung der afrikanischen Tragöden Herrn

IRA ALDRIDGE

vom königlichen Coventgardentheater in London,

in Begleitung seiner englischen Gesellschaft.

Die Hauptscenen aus:

MACBETH.

Tragödie von Shakespeare.

Lady Macbeth.	Frau Stauten.
Macbeth.	Herr Ira Aldridge.
Macduff.	Herr Stauten.
Banquo.	Herr Pasitt.
Fleance.	
Lenox.	Herr Rest.

Hierauf:

The Padlock. (Das Vorlegeschloß.)

Vaudeville in 1 Akt, von Isaac Bickerstaff.

Don Diego.	Herr Stephanus.
Leander.	Herr Stauten.
Mungo.	Herr Ira Aldridge.
Leonore.	Frau Stauten.

Herr Ira Aldridge zeichnet in der für ihn geschriebenen Rolle des Mungo, ein naturgetreues Bild des Negersklaven und trägt folgende Lieder vor: „Dear Heart, what a terrible Life I'm led", „Opposum up a Gum Tree" und „Negro Boy".

Zum Schluß: Epilog, gedichtet und gesprochen von Herrn Ira Aldridge.

Vorher (Neu einstudirt):

Ein bengalischer Tiger.

Posse in 1 Akt, nach dem Französischen von C. A. Herrmann.

Regie: Herr von Othegraven.

Robert Schwarz.	Herr Mentel.
Aurelie, seine Frau.	Fräul. Schäfer.
Lisette, ihr Kammermädchen.	Frau Günther-Bachmann.
Gottlieb Fietlich.	Herr von Othegraven.

Ort der Handlung: Berlin.

Freibillets sind ohne Ausnahme ungültig.

Gewöhnliche Preise der Plätze.

Einlaß um 5 Uhr. — Anfang um 6 Uhr. — Ende um 9 Uhr.

Druck von J. B. Hirschfeld in Leipzig.

Playbill from Leipzig, Germany, in 1852, announcing Ira Aldridge playing the roles of Macbeth and Mungo

Aldridge visited Poland five times, all during a period when it was being ruled by several other countries. There were frequent uprisings of the people to gain independence, which could be seen as a parallel to the anti-slavery movement. When Aldridge went to Warsaw in May 1862, he deliberately performed with Polish speaking actors and he was referred to as "our brother".

One uprising against Russian rule began in 1863, which was finally crushed in 1864, after 18 months fighting, in which 25,000 Poles were killed. When Aldridge returned in 1867, there is evidence that he was under close surveillance by the Russian police because he was suspected of sympathising with the Polish resistance movement.

Tour of Russia

"Moscow university students, thrilled by his acting, unhitched his horses and themselves pulled his carriage through the streets."
Roi Ottley *Black Odyssey: The Story of the Negro in America* 1949

"At the time Gautier saw Aldridge in St. Petersburg, conditions were such in the United States that the great actor could have been claimed as a fugitive slave, arrested by a U.S. marshal, and rushed to the Deep South where he would have been driven to work with whips."
Abner W. Berry *Ira Aldridge: A Negro Actor's Triumph* 1954

"The Russian and Polish responses to his acting demonstrate that in the nineteenth century Aldridge, as a mere 'Negro', was not only one of the best and most effective emissaries of Shakespeare, but also a compelling representative of the antislavery movement and an effective ambassador for the politically, socially, and culturally abused."
Krystyna Kujawinska Courtney 2006

In 1858 he made his first tour of Russia and a Russian commentator, K. Zvantsev, remarked on its political significance: "In our contemporary history there is an event which creates a whole sphere of life and thought, i.e. the liberation of the Negro in the United States; this becomes

Ira Aldridge as Othello in Moscow

something *internal*, not only for the enslaved people, but for all of us. That is why for us, at this particular time, the role of Othello performed by this artist of genius, with all its subtleties of tribal and climatic character, has a universal mighty significance. From Othello is torn the deep cry 'Oh misery, misery, misery!' and in that misery of the African artist is heard the far-off groans of his own people, oppressed by unbelievable slavery and more than that – the groans of the whole of suffering mankind."

Harriet Beecher Stowe

Zvantsev concluded: "Seeing before us the tamed Othello in the net of the tamer, seeing the wild lion in the power of the educated European (the Iago of contemporary history), one involuntarily thinks of the many generations of black people suffering under the whip of American slave-traders."

A few years earlier, in 1852, Harriet Beecher Stowe's *Uncle Tom's Cabin, or Negro Life in the Slave States of America* had been published and within ten years had been translated into 23 languages. (The Polish translation in 1853 had coincided with Aldridge's tour of Poland.) Before the end of 1852 there were already at least three

**Cruickshank illustration for an 1853
edition of *Uncle Tom's Cabin***

dramatisations of the book being performed in
London theatres. At one point, four different stage
versions were playing in New York, another twelve
in London, and countless others around the world.
It remained America's most popular play for eighty
years after its publication.

The author had no first-hand experience of
slavery in the South, but relied on the information
supplied by fugitive slaves, in particular Josiah
Henson who visited her on a number of
occasions. Henson was born into slavery in

Josiah Henson

Charles County, Maryland, in 1789. He escaped to Canada in 1830 where he founded a settlement and school for other fugitive slaves. In 1849 his autobiography *The Life of Josiah Henson* was first published, written from his dictation. He helped with the Underground Railroad and also spoke at anti-slavery meetings in England. One visit he made to England was to the Great Exhibition of 1851. He brought with him some boards of highly polished black walnut, from his saw-mill in Canada, for which he received a bronze medal. He met Queen Victoria whom he heard asking: "Is he indeed a fugitive slave?"

The Great Exhibition in the Crystal Palace, Hyde Park, 1851

The fact that he was the only black exhibitor in the whole of the Crystal Palace reveals the state of Victorian England in which Aldridge was acting. Henson found it "saddening", as he reflected ironically: "But among all the exhibitors from every nation in Europe, and from Asia, and America, and the Isles of the Sea, there was not a single black man but myself. There were negroes there from Africa, brought to be exhibited, but no exhibitors but myself."

Uncle Tom's Cabin galvanised world opinion against slavery and was particularly popular in Russia, where people could easily see the parallels with serfdom. The Russian writer Nikolay Chernyshevsky, in his novel *A Vital Question; or What is to be Done*, declared: "I am for the illiterate blacks against their civilised slave-owners."

Ira Aldridge as King Lear

Ira Aldridge as Shylock

**Playbill announcing a performance of *Othello*
in Kharkov, 1865**

Théophile Gautier, the French poet and
novelist, saw Aldridge act in St. Petersburg and
commented on the "stupendous effect" which he
produced: "We considered him better in the part of
the old King, pestered by his spiteful daughters,

than he was in the Moor of Venice. In the former he acted; in Othello he was just himself." He adds further praise for his performance as King Lear: "Although robust and in the prime of life, Ira Aldridge, during the whole evening, did not make one youthful action; his voice, step, and gestures were all those of an eighty-year-old."

Gautier also describes Aldridge's 'whiting up' for the part: "A flesh-coloured headpiece of papier maché, from which hung some silvery locks of hair, covered his woolly thatch and came down almost to his eyebrows like a helmet; an addition of wax filled in the curves of his flat nose. A thick coat of grease paint covered his black cheeks, and a great white beard enveloped the rest of his face and came down over his chest."

One Russian critic said that the evenings on which he saw Aldridge's Othello, Lear, Shylock and Macbeth "were undoubtedly the best that I have ever spent in the theatre". His productions of *Macbeth* and *Richard III* were the first ever in Russia. His interpretation of Shylock was particularly impressive, portrayed as an outcast from society, persecuted because of his race. In one Russian town a delegation of local Jews officially thanked him for his sympathetic portrayal.

Another critic wrote: "After Aldridge, it is impossible to see Othello performed by a white actor, be it Garrick himself." The famous Russian actor Sosnitsky said: "I have never seen in my life such a talent and I have never dreamed of one like that. It is really astonishing what heights a genius can reach."

The Russian historian Mikhail Pogodin added his praise: "He speaks a language that we do not understand, but the power of his soul is so great and so great is the power of his art that he conquers you the first time you meet him. In the farce The Padlock, when the savage master raised his stick over the head of the downtrodden Negro, I just saw one thing – one shudder running through his spine and his shoulder, such a shudder that sent a shudder through my body."

A measure of his star status was the fact that he was paid the equivalent of £60 for each performance. This was about as much as a Russian actor earned for four months' work. He was also provided with accommodation and a coach at government expense.

In 1858 he also acted Othello, Richard III and Macbeth in Serbia. This was the first time Shakespeare had been performed in the country and a plaque was erected in the National Theatre in Belgrade dedicated to the African Roscius.

Acting Style and Politics

"Let your own discretion be your tutor: suit the action to the word, the word to the action; with this special observance, that you o'erstep not the modesty of nature."
Hamlet, in Shakespeare's *Hamlet* 1602

"The weight of this sad time we must obey; Speak what we feel, not what we ought to say."
Albany, in Shakespeare's *King Lear* 1605

"Break your chains and live as brothers."
Taras Shevchenko (1814-1861)

Ira Aldridge had developed a realistic acting style, a contrast with the more usual bombastic, exaggerated method of many nineteenth-century actors. In Russia this was eventually to lead to the Stanislavski (1863-1938) system of acting, naturally portraying a character's emotions, which became a great influence in the twentieth century.

An example of how convincing Aldridge could be is recorded by a Russian actress about her aunt, who played Desdemona to his Othello in Kharkov and Kiev. She was so frightened in the murder scene that he had to whisper reassurance: "Suddenly in her ear she heard Aldridge whispering in Russian, 'Nichevo, Nichevo' (It's all right. It's all right). And then he continued in English – in a burst of rage. His hands gripped her

by the throat. He is smothering her with the pillow. Before her that terrible face, in a flash that whisper, 'Nichevo; nye boysya' (It's all right; don't be frightened). Neither the public, nor even the actors standing in the wings, overcome by the acting of the tragedian, noticed anything. At the end of the act, a storm of applause. And still trembling from the terror she had experienced, poor Desdemona came out hand-in-hand with the 'black monster', who was now calmly smiling at her."
(*The Path of a Provincial Actress*, M. I. Belizary)

A Russian cartoon showed Aldridge, as Othello, shaking the actor who was playing Iago. Another showed him before a judge, with Desdemona.

> *DESDEMONA*: Save me! This savage one day will really suffocate me!
> *JUDGE*: You must be more careful, Mr. Othello. If you do actually suffocate her, what will happen then?
> *OTHELLO*: Nichevo. Just you give me another Desdemona better than this one.

Aldridge also introduced new ways of rehearsing, politely assembling the actors and calling them by the parts they were going to play. He got to know them and, when leaving, said, "I hope to see you in the best of health." Such manners were unknown in the theatre at that time. Actors would come to his productions to learn more about their theatrical art.

Aldridge's performances had a political effect in Russia. In 1861 the movement for social reform

Cartoon from *Son of the Fatherland*, Russia, 1858, showing Ira Aldridge as Othello shaking Iago

Cartoon from *Son of the Fatherland*, Russia 1858, showing Ira Aldridge before the judge with Desdemona

ACTING STYLE AND POLITICS

had led to the emancipation of the serfs, who could be sold like slaves by their landlords. Ten million male peasants and their families were granted their freedom. Oppression and state censorship continued however and both *Macbeth* and *King Lear* were banned. In one the king is murdered and in the other he goes mad! By 1864 Aldridge was no longer permitted to perform in the capital, St. Petersburg.

Although Aldridge was not overtly involved in the radical political movements of his times, his very presence on the stage was a very powerful political symbol. This was recognised by Taras Shevchenko, the Ukrainian national poet, whom he first met one December evening in St. Petersburg in 1858.

Shevchenko was born a serf in a village near Kiev in 1814 and first worked as a shepherd. His talent at sketching and painting was noticed and encouraged by a group of artists who raised the money to buy his freedom and he became a free man in 1838. In his poetry he criticised the Russian tyranny of the Czars and in 1847 he served a sentence of ten years penal military service.

At one of their meetings, at the home of Count Fyodor Tolstoy, Shevchenko offered to draw a potrait of Aldridge, who was not able to keep still for long. He started making faces, reflecting his misery, and then fell about laughing. Shevchenko angrily stopped his work and Aldridge promptly made a frightened face and sat down quietly

Drawing of Ira Aldridge and Taras Shevchenko by L.O. Pasternak

Drawing of Ira Aldridge in Russia, 1858, by Taras Shevchenko

**Taras Shevchenko,
Ukrainian national poet**

again, but only for a while. Suddenly he asked, "May I sing?" Shevchenko replied, "Oh, you... All right, sing!"

The Count's daughter, Ekaterina, who was fifteen at the time, later recorded in her *Memoirs* what happened next: "Then began a touching, sad Negro melody, which gradually passed into a more lively tempo and ended with a mad jig by Aldridge around the studio. Following that, he would act a whole comic scene (he was an excellent comedian). Taras Grigorievitch was caught up by his merriment and sang Ukrainian

Ira Aldridge as Othello in Odessa, 1866

songs, then became engrossed in conversation about the typical features of different peoples, about the similarity of people, folk lore etc." Despite the diversion, she concluded, "the portrait was finished and turned out to be a lifelike and good resemblance".

She also recalled how moved they were by each other's lives, in which there were obvious similarities. Although she translated some of their longer conversations, she noted: "They understood each other very well: they were both artists, and that meant that they were observant, and both had

Ira Aldridge during his stay in Ukraine

very expressive faces and Aldridge, by gestures and mimicry, could represent everything he wanted to say." This encounter illustrates Aldridge's political sympathies, his cultural interests and his sense of humour and spontaneity.

Once banned from St. Petersburg, Aldridge made several long tours of the Russian provinces, often being the first to bring Shakespeare to the people. One critic wrote from Odessa in 1866: "It is already some years that Aldridge, in the role of a strolling missionary of art, has enlightened the

Russian public with the light of the immortal creations of Shakespeare: at the moment there is not one provincial city, it seems to me, not one well-known fair in Russia, where the light of Shakespeare's genius has not penetrated, thanks to this travelling tragedian."

His journeys were made by stagecoach or horse-sleigh along what he calls "such desperate roads". In a letter from Kybrusk (30 May 1864) he describes how he "caught a bad cough", and his health must certainly have suffered from all these exertions.

Citizenship and Family

"So I was *sold* at last! A human being sold
in the free city of New York! The bill of sale
is on record, and future generations will learn
from it that women were articles of traffic in
New York, late in the nineteenth century of the
Christian religion."
Harriet Jacobs *Incidents in the Life of a Slave
Girl* 1861

"I have been forty years a slave and forty
years free, and would be here forty more years
to have equal rights for all. I suppose I am kept
here because something remains for me to do; I
suppose I am yet to help to break the chain."
Sojourner Truth 1867

Back in England, Aldridge's Certification of
Naturalisation was granted on 7 November 1863.
He wanted this so that he could hold on to his
property and hand it on to his family. Earlier that
year, on 1st January, Abraham Lincoln had issued
the Proclamation of Negro Emancipation. Another
reason for wanting British citizenship may well
have been because Aldridge was thinking of
returning to America.

On 25 March 1864 his wife Margaret died of
"asthma and general debility". According to Ira's
younger daughter "she made him work hard and
was like a mother to him". She also raised Ira's
son Ira Daniel as her own, though nothing is

Sojourner Truth

known about his real mother, except that she was an Irish lady.

In 1860, when they were living in Wellington Road (now Warden Road) Kentish Town, north London, Ira wrote to his friend James McCune Smith: "My son, who has just entered his thirteenth year, is at the Collegiate School of Camden Town, and is a great favourite with his masters, who enter a high opinion of his mental capabilities."

Amanda Brandt

Margaret was completely opposed to her husband going back to America. In the same letter Ira wrote: "Mr. Henry Wallack suggested a visit to America in 1858, but my dear wife would not entertain the idea, her prejudice is so rooted against the Americans for their treatment of our oppressed race generally."

On 20 April, 1865, Ira married Amanda Brandt, a Swedish concert singer, in the parish church in Penge. She was 27 years younger than him and their relationship had probably begun in 1858. She had already borne two children with him, Luranah in 1860 and Frederick in 1862. By this time they had a London home in Hamlet Road, Upper Norwood, near where the Crystal Palace

Abraham Lincoln

had been re-erected. Another daughter, Amanda, was born on 10 March 1866.

He thought again of going back to America for a tour, but although slavery in the USA was ended in 1865 with the conclusion of the Civil War, the prospects for black actors had not improved, as Errol Hill points out: "In 1867 the only roles available to black performers were on the minstrel stage. Interracial casting was non-existent, and there were no black companies with which he could work."

Ira Frederick Olaff Aldridge, Ira's younger son

Nevertheless, with typical bravery, in his final year he did write from Paris authorising theatrical agents in New York to arrange for his appearance "in such cities and towns which you think it will be prudent for me to visit". A tentative date was set and he was expected to leave for New York on 16 August 1867.

While in Paris, after a tour of 35 French towns, Aldridge met Hans Christian Andersen, an encounter recorded in Andersen's autobiography *The Mermaid Man*: "One day as I was walking

Ira Aldridge during his stay in Kiev, 1866

along, a smartly dressed woman came up with her husband, a Negro, and accosted me in a mixture of Swedish, English and German. She had been born in Sweden, but had spent many years abroad. She said that she knew me from my portrait and wished to present her husband who proved to be that excellent Negro actor Ira Aldridge, then drawing the Parisians to the Odeon Theatre where he was playing Othello. We shook hands and exchanged a few politenesses in English. I admit that it pleased me to have one of Africa's gifted sons hail me as a friend."

At this time Aldridge may have realised that he was quite seriously ill, because on 25 June he made his will. He left everything to his wife, except for £500 which he bequeathed to his son Ira Daniel "on his attaining the age of twenty-five years".

Death and Funeral

"A Military Band accompanied the funeral, which played the hymn from Haydn's Oratorio, as well as the Society of Singers, in uniform, and the Society of Dramatic Artists under the direction of Mr N. Hentschel. On the front of the coffin were carried his Orders on a cushion and the deceased was decorated with a laurel wreath. Behind the hearse followed the President of the City of Lodz, a Military Guard of Honour, and Guilds with their banners. The widow rode in a carriage at the end of the procession."
Warsaw Courier Number 182

"Let four captains
Bear Hamlet, like a soldier, to the stage;
For he was likely had he been put on,
To have proved most royally; and, for his pasage,
The soldiers' music and the rites of war
Speak loudly for him."
Fortinbras, in Shakespeare's *Hamlet* 1602

After his performances in Paris, and prior to his planned visit to New York, Ira was invited to play Othello in Lodz, Poland, but fell ill with a lung infection and on 7 August he died, aged 60. According to the *Warsaw Courier*, "a boil on the breast opened up, which proved fatal to him, and though they called in seven of the most eminent doctors in the city, they could not save him". He "passed away peacefully and painlessly", with his wife at his side. His death was reported all round

Ira Aldridge's Grave in Lodz, Poland

Irene Luranah Aldridge, Ira's elder daughter

the world, for example in London, Vienna, St. Petersburg, Chicago and in Melbourne where his elder son heard about it.

A state funeral was arranged. The *Warsaw Courier* reported: "On the 9th of this month there took place the burial of Ira Aldridge, the Negro dramatic actor, in the Evangelical Cemetery of the City of Lodz. The day before the funeral, the Society of Singers of that city, made up of more than one hundred and twenty people, bade farewell to him in song."

Portrait of Ira Aldridge as Othello, on his tombstone in Lodz

In May 1890 a grand concert was organised in Lodz by artists of Poland and Germany to raise funds for a tombstone to be erected on the grave. His elder daughter Luranah, who was a contralto singer at Covent Garden, also took part. The grave is still cared for by the Lodz Appreciation Society and many other citizens of the city who regularly decorate it with fresh flowers and lit candles.

Of his five children, Ira Daniel emigrated to Australia, Frederick became a musician, Luranah and Amanda were both concert singers, and Rachel, born a few months after her father's death, died in infancy.

Reputation

**"Othello's occupation's gone – 'tis o'er,
The mask has fallen, I'm your actor here no more."**
Ira Aldridge *Farewell Address*

**"Few Americans except students of the
specialized history of the theatre know much
about the New York-born Negro who from 1833
until his death in 1867 was the world's most
celebrated interpreter of Shakespeare."** Abner W.
Berry *Ira Aldridge: A Negro Actor's Triumph* 1954

**"Aldridge is forgotten in the British Isles where
he built his reputation as an actor of world
stature and in the United States of America
where he was born."** Owen Mortimer *Speak of Me
as I Am: The Story of Ira Aldridge* 1995

A year before Aldridge died, another Black American actor, born in Philadelphia, arrived in England with his wife and small child. His name was Samuel Morgan Smith and he was to carry on where Aldridge had left off.

Within days of his arrival he had a contract to manage a little theatre in Gravesend, where he performed the roles of Richard III, Macbeth, Hamlet, Shylock and Othello. His wife died the following year, aged 27, and he later married an English actress. He toured the country with her for the next 13 years, but after an early retirement, died of pneumonia at his home in Sheffield, aged forty-nine.

Samuel Morgan Smith

Both Ira Aldridge and Samuel Smith were soon forgotten. For a hundred years or more, after Aldridge's death, books were written on nineteenth-century English theatre without a single mention of him! He was hidden from history, just like Mary Seacole. Some American actors, however, kept Ira's name alive and, at the end of the nineteenth century, a number of Black amateur theatre companies in the USA adopted Aldridge's name. In 1920 a playhouse in Oklahoma City was also established called the Aldridge Theatre.

In 1932 the new Shakespeare Memorial Theatre at Stratford-upon-Avon was officially opened. The old theatre had burned down and a world-wide campaign for funds was launched.

Shakespeare Memorial Theatre, Stratford-upon-Avon

Nearly a quarter of a million pounds was raised, almost half coming from America. The poet James Weldon Johnson presented a gift from "the Negroes of the United States" and a bronze plate was attached to one of the seats in the theatre bearing the inscription – IRA ALDRIDGE. Thirty-two other actors were also honoured, including Richard Burbage, David Garrick, Edmund Kean and Ellen Terry.

There is a direct link between Ira Aldridge and the other most famous Black actor who played Othello, Paul Robeson. Ira's daughter Amanda was a singer and teacher, as well as a composer under the name of Montague Ring. In 1930 she gave elocution lessons to Robeson as he was

Seat commemorating Ira Aldridge in the Shakespeare Memorial Theatre, Stratford-upon-Avon

preparing for his first appearance as Othello, with Peggy Ashcroft as Desdemona, at the Savoy Theatre in London.

Robeson mentioned this in a BBC broadcast, which was carried in America by the Columbia Broadcasting System, explaining how Amanda had helped him to prepare his interpretation of the part. The production created a stir in America and Robeson hoped to take the play to New York in October of that year. But as with Ira Aldridge a hundred years earlier, racism got in the way and Paul Robeson did not play Othello in New York until thirteen years later, when the play ran for a record 250 performances.

Peggy Ashcroft and Paul Robeson in *Othello*, Savoy Theatre, 1930

John Dover Wilson, the famous Shakespeare scholar, saw the first night of Robeson's performance in London on 19 May, 1930, and it was a revelation to him: "I felt I was seeing the tragedy for the first time, not merely because of Robeson's acting, which despite a few petty faults of technique was magnificent, but because the fact that he was a true Negro seemed to floodlight the whole drama. Everything was slightly different from what I had previously imagined; new points, fresh nuances, were constantly emerging; and all had, I felt, been clearly intended by the author. The performance convinced me, in short, that a Negro

Othello is essential to the full understanding of the play." This must surely have been the response of many of those who saw Aldridge play Othello.

Aldridge's reputation was acknowledged by Robeson when he gave Amanda a photo of himself, on which he wrote: "To Miss Aldridge – With many thanks for the inspiration received from all the reports of her father's greatness. I realise that I can only carry on in the 'tradition of Aldridge'." Amanda died in 1956, the day before her ninetieth birthday, and is buried in Streatham Cemetery, in London.

Paul Robeson was loved and admired by the Russian people in the same way in which Ira Aldridge had been. Aldridge was even put forward as an example to the Red Army in their epic war against Nazi Germany. In 1942 Mikhail Morozov, a professor at the University of Moscow, was relating the story of Aldridge's struggle to Soviet soldiers who were commemorating the 75th anniversary of Aldridge's death and said: "The spiritual and humane character of Aldridge's art is especially near and comprehensible to us in these dark days of our struggle with an enemy attempting to enslave the world, an enemy striking for that kingdom of darkness against which Ira Aldridge, the great Negro tragedian, had fought, with his magnificent art for a sword."

In 1946, when Robeson was in England again, he discussed the idea of making a film about the life of Ira Aldridge and work was begun on a script. Unfortunately the film did not materialise because

Robeson's passport was taken from him when he returned to the United States and he was not allowed to leave the country. Robeson did play Othello again in England, however, in 1959, directed by Tony Richardson.

One of the most recent Black actors to play Othello is Ray Fearon, who performed in the 1999 Royal Shakespeare Company production, directed by Michael Attenborough. Fearon was born in London in 1967 to Jamaican parents who came to England in the 1950s. He acknowledges his debt to Ira Aldridge: "For me Ira Aldridge has been one of the greatest pioneers of classical acting on the world stage and has been a great inspiration for me in my stage career. It has been an honour to be a part of his on-going legacy of classical acting in the theatre today."

In 2003 Oku Ekpenyon asked the Old Vic if they would put up a portrait of Ira Aldridge in the theatre where he had performed (when it was the Royal Coburg), but with little response. The following year she renewed the campaign with the support of the Black and Asian Studies Association (BASA), sending the executive director of the theatre 382 signatures and sixteen letters of support.

The management finally agreed to display a picture of Aldridge as Aaron in *Titus Andronicus*, donated by the National Portrait Gallery, and the unveiling ceremony took place on 24 September, 2004. Oku's guest at the crowded event was the Bermudian film actor Earl Cameron who, in his

Amanda Ira Aldridge, Ira's younger daughter

speech, recorded his link with Aldridge. In the 1940s, when he was starting out as a theatre actor in London, he had been taught elocution by Aldridge's daughter, Amanda.

In 2007, the 200th anniversary of Aldridge's birth, English Heritage agreed to put up one of their famous blue plaques on the house where he lived in Hamlet Road, Upper Norwood.

Research continues into Ira Aldridge's life. New information is constantly being discovered. We have not heard the last about this extraordinary man.

BIBLIOGRAPHY

Anon (1849) **Memoir and Theatrical Career of Ira Aldridge, the African Roscius**, London: J Onwhyn

Berry, Abner W. (1954) 'Ira Aldridge: A Negro Actor's Triumph', **Masses & Mainstream**, Vol. 7,Number 2

Brown, William Wells (1863) **The Black Man: His Antecedents, His Genius, and His Achievements,** Boston: James Redpath

Courtney, Krystyna Kujawinska (2006) 'Ira Aldridge, Shakespeare, and Color-Conscious Performances in Nineteenth-Century Europe', in Thompson, Ayanna (ed.) **Colorblind Shakespeare**, New York: Routledge

Hay, Samuel A. (1994) **African American Theatre,** Cambridge: Cambridge University Press

Hill, Errol (1984) **Shakespeare in Sable: A History of Black Shakespearean Actors**, Amherst: University of Massachusetts Press

Hill, Errol G. & Hatch, James V. (2003) **A History of African American Theatre**, Cambridge: Cambridge University Press

Lindfors, Bernth (1994) 'Nothing extenuate, nor set down aught in malice: new biographical information on Ira Aldridge', **African American Review**, Volume 28, Number 3

Malone, Mary (1969) **Actor in Exile: The Life of Ira Aldridge**, New York: Crowell-Collier Press

Marshall, Herbert & Stock, Mildred (1958) **Ira Aldridge: The Negro Tragedian**, London: Rockcliff

Martineau, Harriet (1837) **Society in America,** London: Saunders & Otley

Mortimer, Owen (1995) **Speak of Me as I Am: The Story of Ira Aldridge**, Wangaratta, Victoria, Australia: The Author

Scobie, Edward (1972) **Black Britannia – A History of Blacks in Britain**, Chicago: Johnson Publishing Company

Smith, James McCune (1860) 'Ira Aldridge', **Anglo-African Magazine**, January

Waters, Hazel (2003) 'Aldridge and the Battlefield of Race', **Race & Class**, Volume 45, Number 1

Waters, Hazel (2007) **Racism on the Victorian Stage**, Cambridge: Cambridge University Press

Wordson, Carter G. (1922) **The Negro in Our History**, Washington: Associated Publishers